THE COMPLETE GUIDE TO CONDUCTING SEMINARS AT SEA

1/3/2

Katrina,
To the one who see's all things my way! And, to one (one) who knows me only too well!
All my love,
Mary.

THE COMPLETE GUIDE TO

CONDUCTING SEMINARS AT SEA

Mary Long

Athina Press

The Complete Guide To Conducting Seminars At Sea
Copyright © 1999 by Mary Long. All rights reserved. Printed in the United States of America. No part of this book may be used or reproduced in any manner whatsoever without written permission except in the case of brief quotations embodied in critical articles and reviews.
For information address:
Athina Press Publishing
1630 S.E. Rex St.
Portland, OR 97202
Phone: 503.232.5362
Fax: 503.232.1952
Email: MaryLong@SeminarAtSea.com
Website: http://www.SeminarAtSea.com

FIRST EDITION

Cover design by Marcy Rouske

Long, Mary.
    The Complete Guide To Conducting Seminars At Sea: for speakers, consultants, trainers in any profession taking their business to the high seas aboard the luxury liners of the world

ISBN 0-9666733-0-1

Athina Press Publishing
A Division of Travel Resource Center, Inc.

This book is dedicated to my husband Paul,
THE most special person in the world

Acknowledgments

Several years ago when I conducted my first seminar at sea I asked myself the question "Does it really get any better than this?" *The Complete Guide to Conducting Seminars At Sea* is testimony to the extraordinary opportunities awaiting the tens of thousands of seminar professionals and others who would like to share their expertise with the world. I am thrilled to share my experience, knowledge, and practical tips so that you too can participate in the abundance seminaring at sea offers. I know that if you have even a fraction of the joy I have experienced, you will be hooked on cruising for life.

Many people have contributed importantly to this project and I want to especially acknowledge the following:

Dr. Lynda C. Falkenstein, "The Niche Doctor" and author of internationally acclaimed *NICHECRAFT: Using Your Specialness to Focus Your Business, Corner Your Market, and Make Customers Seek You Out*; Mr. Gary Fee, President, OSSN (Outside Sales Support Network and Travel Support System, Inc.); dear friend, Marci Dickinson, owner of Take Off Kits; Lora Abernathy, American Hawaii Cruises; John McEvroy, Entertainment Director, Radisson 7 Seas Cruises;

Kirk Frederick, Entertainment Director, Crystal Cruises, Seabourn Cruises; Kathy Owens, former Director Of Sales, Princess Cruises; David Stewartson, Entertainment Director, Cunard Line Cruises; Officer Leslie Hockett, Social Hostess, Sky Princess, Princess Cruises; Mr. Tom Janaky, former Sales Manager of American Hawaii Cruises; Rich Skinner, former Director of Public Relations, Holland America Cruise Lines; Katherine Horandi, owner of Wild Katz Designs; Tricia B. Samson, Assistant to the President, American Canadian Caribbean Line, Inc.; Elizabeth Raven McQuinn, Director of Public Relations, Clipper Cruise Lines; Carrie Hosmer, Marketing Coordinator, Cape Canaveral Cruise Line; Michael Lomax, Executive VP/General Manager, America West Steamboat Co.; Jan Myers, Gillies & Zaiser Public Relations Firm for Bergen Line/Norwegian Coastal Voyages; Quari Pandya, Marketing/Communications Coordinator, Costa Cruise Lines N.V; Marla Moran, Public Relations Dept. & David Stewartson, Entertainment Manager, Cunard Line; Lucille Hostabjian, LMH Communications Seminar Facilities Dept. for EuropeAmerica/Peter Dielmann Cruises; Janis Goller, Public Relations Dept.; Holland America Line; Lynn Mitchell, Assistant Manager of Cruise Programs, Royal Caribbean International; Scott Higashi, Convention Dept., American Hawaii Cruises; Joe McGrath, Entertainment Manager, Commodore Cruise Lines; Steve Hirshan, Vice President of Sales and Marketing, Mediterranean Cruise Lines; Floyd Fickle, Public Relations Coordinator, Alaska Sightseeing West; Jackie Hughett, Public Relations Coordinator, Carnival Cruise Lines; Staff aboard the prestigious Radisson & Seas Cruise *Paul Gauguin*; Hal Fraser,

Entertainer; Oliver Hammerer, Hotel Manager; Margaret McNiff, Social Hostess; and Mark Landon, author, *Cruise Ship Crews – Everything You Need To Know To Get A Cruise Ship Job.*

Table of Contents

Content	Page
PART ONE	
Seminaring at Sea - Its Time Has Come	1
Every Cruise a Unique Experience	2
Endless Advantages	3
Earning $$ and Free Cruises at the Same Time	4
Travel Agents Receive Generous Commissions	5
You, Too, Can Cash in on Group-Travel Profits	5
Treated Like Royalty	6
Am I a Candidate for Seminaring at Sea??	7
Consider Your Audience	9
Bottom-Line Check List	10
Getting on Board – Options and Decisions	12
Self and Co-Sponsored Programs	13
Invited Speaker Program	14
Tips to Increase Your Chances of Getting Hired by a Cruise Line	15
Association or Club Sponsorship	16
Booking Agents: Their Role and What They Mean to You	17
Cruise Lines Direct	19
At Sea at Last - What to Expect	19
Dinner - The Main Event	23
Choosing Your Dinner Hour	23
Seating by the Rules	24

Content	Page
The Seminar Schedule	25
Choosing Your Destination, Itinerary, and Cruise Line	29
Other Considerations When Choosing Your Destination	30
Cruise Line Contacts	37
Marketing Strategies That Produce Sell-Out Crowds	42
YOU'RE IT!	52
The Ultimate Fund-Raising Experience	56
Counting the Money	59
Where the Profit Is	61
Additional Revenue and Profit Opportunities	63
On-Board Gratuities	66
Frequently Asked Questions	69
Your Seminaring-at-Sea Vocabulary	77

PART TWO

Cruise Ship Profiles, Deck Plans, & Photo Gallery	85

Preface

Welcome to the exciting world of seminaring at sea, teaching and lecturing on the high seas, aboard some of the greatest luxury liners in the world. Regardless of your age or occupation you, too, can now combine your passions for travel and speaking AND get paid for it. Although I have personally experienced the joys of seminaring at sea nearly one hundred different times, this book is not about how wonderful my own life has been sailing and lecturing aboard five-star cruise ships. Nor is it about visiting exotic ports and making a living at doing what I love. Instead, its exclusive purpose is providing you enough information so that you, too, can take your own speaking and/or seminar business to sea and make a tidy profit at the same time.

As you read this guidebook, you will doubtless sense my own zeal for this subject. The truth is, after years of professional speaking and seminaring both on land and

> *If you can seminar on land, you can do the same thing aboard a floating hotel at sea.*

at sea, I can say hands down that conducting programs on the high seas offers an unparalled experience. If you are wondering what it would be like for you, start by imagining yourself on a *working vacation*.

Imagine conducting your seminar or presentation on board a floating luxury resort taking you to places you have only dreamed of going. What could possibly be a better combination with so many rewards?? So, if you liked the image of yourself combining lecture and deck chairs, it's time to learn specifically how you can take your own seminars to sea.

Part One

It Doesn't Get Any Better Than This!

Seminaring at Sea - Its Time Has Come

With arrival of the jet-age and today's hurried lifestyles, everything around us seems to move at an almost jarringly fast pace. Life at sea, on the other hand, moves much slower, allowing us to shed our staid demeanors, relax more quickly, and enjoy our lives even more so. For those of us in the seminar and speaking business, the really good news is that today's cruise ships aren't just packing luxury. They are also filled with amenities and services rivaling any major hotel or land-based conference center. It should come as no surprise, then, that conducting significant seminars and conferences on cruise ships has gained huge popularity among American and international businesses.

One of the most attractive features of a cruise to passengers is that it is *all inclusive*. That is, there is no constant dipping into your pocket to pay for meals, snacks, rental cars, and entertainment. As a passenger you have everything paid for when you buy your ticket. As a seminar presenter this is particularly meaningful, because your participants can focus on what you are offering and not worry about details related to their travel. Many times passengers find that cruising is very cost-effective which is extra good news for you. They get so much wrapped into their ticket, paying for your program is barely noticeable. You are part of a glorious package. So, seminaring-at-sea turns out to be the best of all worlds for passenger and presenter.

Every Cruise a Unique Experience

Although I have been on scores of cruises, I still experience a combination of shivers and an almost intoxicating feeling before each sailing. As eager as I am to start my seminar, I am equally excited to meet my new audience and new ship which will be my floating home-office for the next week. I always know that once I set foot onboard ship, I am waving goodbye to the dull and drab land-based conference rooms at home ready to experience a new and very special world.

Your Notes

Endless Advantages

Speaking and seminaring at sea has a host of advantages for professional presenters over conventional land-based venues. Some of them include:

- You have a captive audience. In other words, your audience isn't going to go off for a long walk and forget to come back. Neither are they likely to get lost in some strange city or unfamiliar place.
- Your program is usually broken up into bite-size or manageable chunks, meaning you are not working straight through the day. This ensures you will be able to enjoy the trip, as well.
- Increasing numbers of trade and professional associations are recognizing the advantages of offering travel-education to their members. They can educate their people and use the experience as a revenue center at the same time.
- Free travel opportunities are available to you. For example, in groups which you put together, one person goes free for every 15 paid passengers.

Your Notes

- Cruise lines pay cooperative advertising dollars to help with your promotional efforts.
- High safety and security measures protect you and your property.
- You receive special recognition as a speaker or presenter from the passengers and crew.
- Fresh "salt" sea air during coffee breaks!

Earning $$ and Free Cruises at the Same Time

By participating in the seminar-at-sea process, you are involving yourself in the worlds largest industry, travel and tourism. Most importantly, the specific aspect that you are going to participate in is also the most lucrative part of the industry. Cruise companies aggressively cultivate travel agents, meeting planners and group leaders to help them bring groups on board their vessels. In order for you to receive maximum benefit from your own negotiations with travel agents and other travel-industry professionals, it's important for you to know a little how the business works, including how travel agents are paid.

The next several pages offer insights that will make your own seminar-at-sea experiences more fun and profitable.

Your Notes

Travel Agents Receive Generous Commissions

Cruise companies pay sizable commissions to travel agents for selling their cruises. The standard commission is 10% of the retail ticket price. The real profit is in the group market where the commissions can be much higher. They are paid in what is called *override* commissions for groups. Additionally, travel agents receive one free airline ticket and sea berth (air/sea ticket) for every 15 paid passengers within a set group. These freebies are called "TC's" short for tour conductor tickets.

You, Too, Can Cash in on Group-Travel Profits

I have earned countless air/sea tickets allowing me to:

- Give the tickets to my family members, travel companions or other group participants
- Sell the tickets to use the profit to pay for promotional expenses or use the profit as cash to offset my shopping spree in the exotic ports!

Your Notes

Treated Like Royalty

Aside from making good money when offering your seminars at sea, you receive the special bonus of additional recognition and respect. Passengers think you have a wonderful job working for the cruise line. The captain and crew view you as a unique professional who knows a good thing when you see it. Most of all, a rich bond often develops between you, the passengers, and crew.

As a seminar presenter or speaker it is not unusual to be invited to one of many of the Captain's private cocktail parties. You may even receive a special invitation to be the Captain's dinner guest along with a few other select passengers. One of the social hostess's duties is to scout out who is who on the cruise. You will have the opportunity to meet her early on in the voyage because she is the one supervising all the special events occurring on board. She is the captain's right hand person!

I am almost always invited to the Captain's parties and dinner table at least one night of each voyage.

Your Notes

Sample Dinner Invitation

REGENCY CRUISES

Captain Chronis Verdaridis
Cordially invites

Ms. Long
To Dinner

Caravell Dining Room Aft
at 8:15 on 19 June 93
Please confirm at Pursers Office by 3:00

Treated as royalty, you will be summoned from your stateroom and escorted by his Chief of Staff through the dining room to the Captain's table. You are now viewed as an elite member of this floating community. I always get a kick out of announcing to my tablemates I will not be at our usual table for dinner this evening because I've been invited by the "big guy" to his table and must attend. After all, this *is* protocol!

Am I a Candidate for Seminaring at Sea??

Pack your bags. Almost any topic can put you on a cruise ship. Of course, there are subjects more popular

Your Notes

than others that will cause cruise lines to sign you up fast. And the most popular seminar-at-sea presenters do share some common traits. The following section outlines features of most sought-after presenters, most popular topics, and the kinds of groups likely to utilize programs at sea.

Most sought-after presenters include:

- Speakers/lecturers
- Consultants
- Writers, authors
- Educators
- Trainers
- Planners
- Celebrities, Personalities
- Clergy/Ministry

Hot topics include:

- Health & fitness-related issues
- Athletics, sports
- Beauty & fashion
- Photography & photo journalism
- Financial, investment & retirement planning

Your Notes

- Cooking, cuisine, food & wine
- Computer industry products & technologies
- Computer and internet training, basic skills and advanced
- Home & gardening
- Fine arts, including music, dance, theater, art

Although the range of potential topics is huge, it is clear that those most in demand fall into the human interest areas such as personal and professional enrichment. Other favorites include topics from zoology, art, archeology, architecture, culture, and history.

And a final category which nearly all cruise ships seek out is the expert who can talk about the culture, history, and geography of the region(s) visited during the cruise.

Consider Your Audience

One important way of determining if you have a topic that may "land" you on a cruise ship, is to consider who your typical audience might be. Following is a list of categories of groups and/or professions most often using cruising as a meeting venue:

Your Notes

- Education workshops, clinics, continuing education units
- Corporate incentive programs
- Company award/reward programs
- Business meetings, conferences, trade shows
- Medical industry
- Alumni reunions
- Fund-raisers & charities
- Study tours of all kinds
- Fraternal organizations, clubs, chapters
- Banking, finance
- Retiree's

Bottom-Line Check List

If you have any one or all of the following, then *pack your bags*! You are a candidate for seminaring at sea.

- High-level expertise on a topic of interest to a cruise audience
- Considerable speaking experience and presentation skills
- Audience recognition as an expert in your field
- Ability to comfortably relate to a range of people

Your Notes

⚙ *Special Note:*

When conducting your programs at sea, your responsibilities are somewhat different than those on dry land. As on dry land, you are there to conduct business and then enjoy leisure time. On the other hand, your audience is there primarily to enjoy themselves and pick up business or other information as a secondary experience. While you must meet the latter expectations, you absolutely must satisfy the former. As you consider whether seminaring at sea is your cup of tea, keep in mind that you will be unusually visible throughout your trip. That means passengers and your seminar participants will feel they have access to you anytime they want. And for the most part, they should. While you will definitely set boundaries about your own private time and space, you will be sharing much more of yourself at sea than at land. If this isn't something you feel comfortable with, I suggest that you buy your own ticket and cruise as a passenger, not a presenter.

Your Notes

Getting on Board – Options and Decisions

As you are finding out, planning a successful seminar-at-sea experience requires more than knowing you like to cruise. It means you have to know yourself very well. It also means you must know WHY you are doing your program on board a ship and what you expect to get from it. For example, are you doing it primarily for earned income as you would be on land? Or are you looking to the cruise as a trade, a way to offset your travel experience. In other words, do you simply want to get a free cruise in return for conducting your program on board the ship. Whatever your answer, it's ok. The issue is, you must ask the questions in advance because how you go about marketing your program and the very kind of program you create will be a function of your initial purpose.

Although there may be different combinations of options, the following are the most common ways you have available to get your programs to sea.
They include:
- Self sponsorship
- Association sponsorship
- Invited guest of the cruise line

Your Notes

Within these three categories are subcategories of speakers who are paid a professional fee and those who do their work exclusively as a trade for travel. Now we will look closely at each of these groups with their respective pros and cons in the next several pages.

As we review each of these categories, think carefully about your own needs and the arrangement that will best address your situation.

Self and Co-Sponsored Programs

If total control is your priority, self-sponsorship is the direction you should seriously consider. Self-sponsorship means you will be taking responsibility for getting the program paid for, whether from your own pocket or from the registration fees of those who sign-up. You gather your own flock and see that all bills are paid. You will organize the entire experience from beginning to end. The buck for everything related to the program stops with you.

Your Notes

The following short self-test will help you determine if self-sponsorship is for you:

Your Qualifying Quiz (circle yes or no)

1. Can I draw enough people with my seminar topic to make this a profitable venture?   *yes   no*
2. Can my topic(s) be spread over a multitude of days?   *yes   no*
3. Is my topic sufficiently interesting and unique to draw people?   *yes   no*
4. Do I have the finances to successfully promote this?   *yes   no*
5. Do I have a system in place to effectively market and promote the program?   *yes   no*
6. Do I have sufficient name familiarity to collect enough participants?   *yes   no*
7. Do I want the responsibility of managing, indeed "dealing" with diverse personalities and staff over an extended period of time?   *yes   no*

Invited Speaker Program

Under this program, the cruise line itself invites and most often compensates you for your work. Not surpris-

---

Your Notes

ingly, this is the choice of choices for most presenters. Basically you get invited, show-up, do your work, and get paid. Many times you get paid very well. The cruise line produces the audience, they do all the nitty-gritty, and you have only one responsibility: to "edu-tain" the guests. It is important to emphasize that even though you may be paid very well it is not usually in cash, instead the cruise lines usually will provide one or more of the following:

- Free cruise for you and a companion
- Free round-trip transportation to the ship for you and your companion
- Pay you a speaker fee

In some cases you will be required to pay a nominal $40 room and board fee, though this like most other things is negotiable.

Tips to Increase Your Chances of Getting Hired by a Cruise Line

- Demonstrate excellent communication skills, an engaging personality, upbeat attitude with a

---

Your Notes

- casual demeanor with superb etiquette and manners at all times.
- Have a well-prepared press kit describing your audience and target markets. Include photos and perhaps a recent video.
- Reference your website where you will have your entire program and complete information introducing what you offer, where you've been, and responses from your audience. You may have audio/video which your clients can download for review.
- Alert the cruise lines you have sent out a press kit and then wait 5-6 weeks before checking on its status and the cruise line's level of interest.
- Be prepared to physically go to their land based office to meet formally with key decision-makers.

Association or Club Sponsorship

If you are finding that doing all the work of self-sponsorship is not your first choice, identifying a strong sponsor may be just the answer. Consider the following pros and cons:

Your Notes

On the plus side
+ Someone else pays to promote you
+ You are usually able to set your own fee
+ Your pay is guaranteed regardless how many people sign up or go on the cruise
+ You have an opportunity to access your sponsor's network, ultimately gaining new contacts

On the minus side
− The sponsor controls the topic and who the speakers are
− You may have other duties assigned, such as recruiting, program design, promotion, materials
− Limited ability to self-promote or to sell your product's, or the sponsor may require a commission on your products
− May be paid only by the number of participants signed up or purchasing product

Booking Agents: Their Role and What They Mean to You

It is very important to remember that entertainers and guest speakers are considered part of the cruise ships

---

Your Notes

entertainment department. Your pay and onboard privileges will vary accordingly. You report and abide by the hotel managements rules and regulations.

Today there are two basic ways to get hired:
1   Find an agent who deals specifically with booking speakers and entertainers.
2   Work with the cruise lines own in-house booking service.

Most cruise lines utilize the services of an outside booking agency. Do not expect that the cruise line will reveal to you which agency they use. They tend to be very private about this matter. Industry protocol says don't even ask. Regardless how you contact your agent, you must send your vita directly to the cruise lines entertainment director. If you pass muster, you will be sent to their booking agent for further consideration. If the agent believes you are a good candidate they will contact you directly. Once hired, expect to pay the 10-15% booking fee. To contact a cruise line or booking agent see my *Directory of Cruise Lines international*, Athina Press.

Your Notes

Cruise Lines Direct

Most people will agree this is the best method to get hired. You deal one-on-one with the entertainment director, avoid a middle person, and don't have to pay a booking fee.

Special Note:

Keep your eye out for theme cruises. Throughout the year, many lines offer theme cruises. Some of them are on an annual basis; others are one-time only events. Many presenters design their programs to coincide specifically with the theme for a particular sailing. This is a very smart strategy because it makes you appear as especially valuable to a given audience at a given time. Find out about the schedule of themes, request that the cruise lines send you their brochures listing various programs for the next year. Travel agencies usually receive this information shortly after the first of the year.

At Sea at Last - What to Expect

You are an expert at your program. That we already know. If you weren't, you wouldn't even be reading this

---

Your Notes

book much less thinking about taking your knowledge to others. What you probably don't know are all the nuances of what to expect when you take yourself and your seminar to sea. This section provides a typical scenario from the time you get on board the cruise liner to the trip's wind down and your disembarkation. As you read through each of these points, consider how they will apply to your situation:

1. As soon as you get on board, safely store all your master seminar materials in your stateroom.
2. Do the same thing with other valuables such as prescription medications and anything that would signal disaster were it lost during your trip.
3. Since the ship usually sails within a few hours after your embarkation, plan to freshen up, change into professional attire, and proceed to the hotel manager's office. They are concerned about your arrival. As you can imagine, they want to make sure all of their presenters are accounted for before anchors are lifted! Announce your arrival to the ship's officers and social hostess ASAP.
4. While in the ship's office, confirm your agenda, making any last-making adjustments. Once that agenda has been cast in the proverbial concrete,

---

Your Notes

you are ready to meet your seminar participants at your welcome-aboard party.

5. Anticipate that somewhere in the first evening of your cruise, there will be a mandatory fire-drill. If you are on a ship that does not have one, you may want to reconsider whether this is a ship you should be on in the first place! Alert your group that first-night fire drills are just that. They should not panic. They are for your safety, and good for photos, too!

6. Make arrangements with the ship's photographer for a group photo. One of the best mementos of any cruise is the group photo. People show it over and over again and keep it for years. It is a great marketing tool for you, as well. You may want to have a small sign to put in front of the group. The sign could have your name, e.g. Mary Long's *Seminar at Sea, Class of 2001!*

7. Consider sponsoring your own welcome-aboard reception party for people in your group. I usually hold this event about an hour and a half before dinner. I include light snacks, and a range of beverages. Some cruise lines charge a per-person

---

Your Notes

8. Know your ship's chain of command. Knowing exactly who reports to who is very important to your smooth sailing. Literally every ship you sail on has the same chain, so getting accustomed to one prepares you for all. Following is the listing of personnel categories and their hierarchy of responsibility and authority:

– Captain
– Chief Officer/Engineers
– Cruise Director
– Hotel Manager
– Social Host or Hostess
– Purser
– Shore Excursion Manager
– Food & Beverage Manager
– Head Chef
– Gift Store Manager
– Room Steward
– Photographer

Your Notes

⚙ *Special Note:*

Negotiate a group photo discount price with the photographer. Lower prices will encourage your group members to buy this important reminder of their great experience with you. Sometimes I provide it as a personal gift to thank the attendees.

Dinner - The Main Event

Dinner is such a major event aboard ship that it deserves a separate section entirely. Shipboard dinners become legends long after cruises end. Conversations about cruises invariably focus, at least for a time, on dinner, dinner, dinner. As with many other aspects of cruising, tradition guides much of the dinner process. If you are a novice at cruising, the following discussion will be particularly helpful.

Choosing Your Dinner Hour

When booking your group cruise you'll be required to choose one of two dinner seating times for everyone in your group. The first or main seating is held from 6-8pm; the later seating goes from 8:30-10pm. I prefer

---

Your Notes

the later time because it gives me more time in port or to run my seminars later in the day without rushing to close down. The more luxurious the cruise, the more open seatings exist. This means you may go to dinner whenever you please, usually between 7-10pm. The same concept applies to breakfast and lunch.

⚙ *Special Note:*

Check out the Lido Deck when you feel like a casual breakfast or lunch. This is especially nice if you don't have time to sit through a full hour of formal dining. The Lido Deck is usually located on the very top outside deck. What a view!

Seating by the Rules

When eating in the dining room or ships restaurant, every person in your group is seated by pre-assignment for the duration of the voyage. This has distinct benefit to you because you are able to visit each table in your group on a regular basis. Usually two nights into the cruise, I'll begin my table hop visiting all attendees. I want each person in my group to know I care about them individually. I also know from experience that participants like to have their group leader demonstrate attention to their needs. They think of you as a celebrity of sorts and feel even more important when you acknowledge their presence.

The Seminar Schedule

The actual seminar or substantive part of your experience is woven throughout the entire trip and takes into account length of stay in ports, length of entire trip, and type of program you are offering. It is important to remember that although they may report otherwise on their tax statements, the truth for most attendees is they are on the cruise first and attending your program second. This is a case where success depends upon you remembering the adage about tail not wagging the dog. In your situation, the cruise is the major player or canine and your seminar is the tail. It's a great tail, but that's what it is. Don't forget it.

Although each program will be different, the following sample schedules will give you an idea how substance and travel can be woven together to make for an exciting and informative experience.

Your Notes

Sample A: Seven-day Agenda

7/23 Sat	2:00pm - 4:00pm	Board ship, check in at SAS desk by 4:00pm
	6:15pm - 7:15pm	Your Welcome Aboard cocktail reception
	Suggested attire:	Semi-formal
7/24 Sun	8:00am - 8:15am	Registration and sign in
	8:15am - 9:00am	Orientation and introductions.
	9:00am - 10:15am	*Your Seminar Part I*
	10:30am - 12:00n	*Your Seminar Part II*
	12:00n - 2:00pm	Lunch on your own
	2:15pm - 4:00pm	*Your Seminar Part III*
	6:15pm - 7:00pm	Captain's Welcome Aboard Cocktail Reception
7/25 Mon	8:00am - 11:00am	Visit St. John
	11:15am - 12:15pm	*Your Seminar Part IV*
	12:15pm - 2:00pm	Lunch on your own
	2:15pm - 3:00pm	*Your Seminar Part V*
	3:00pm - 8:00pm	Visit St. Thomas,

Your Notes

Mary Long

7/26 Tue	9:00am - 11:00am	*Your Seminar Part VI*
	11:00am - 6:00pm	Remainder of day on your own
	6:15pm - 7:15pm	Your cocktail party
	Suggested attire:	Semi-casual

Note: Invite the captain and Chief of Staff to your party

7/27 Wed	9:00am - 10:15am	Your *Seminar Part VII*
	10:30am - 11:00am	*Your Seminar Part VIII*
	11:15am - 11:30am	Group photo session following this morning's seminar
	12:00n - 6:00pm	Visit Aruba, dinner on your own
7/28 Thur	8:00am - 11:00pm	Barbados, full day/night on your own
7/29 Fri	8:15am - 9:15am	*Your Seminar Part IX*
	9:30am - 11:00am	*Your Seminar Part X, closing remarks*
	11:00am - 6:15pm	Rest of day on your own
	6:15pm - 7:00pm	Captain's Farewell Cocktail Reception Dress attire: Formal
7/30 Sat	9:00am - 12:00pm	Disembark ship

Total seminar hours: 14

Your Notes

This sample itinerary will give you additional insights as you plan your own seminar at sea.

Sample B: Seven-day Caribbean Cruise Itinerary

Day	Port	Arrives	Departs
1	Miami		5:00pm
2	*At Sea*		
3	St. John	8:00am	11:00am
	St. Thomas	12:00pm	8:00pm
4	St. Maarten	8:00am	6:00pm
5	Aruba	11:00am	6:00pm
6	Barbados	8:00am	9:00pm
7	*At Sea*		
8	Miami	8:00am	

☸ Special Note:

Sometimes I arrange a swap meet toward the end of the voyage giving everyone a chance to trade or sell things they've purchased in port.

Your Notes

Choosing Your Destination, Itinerary, and Cruise Line

Choosing your destination and figuring out the right itinerary is a very different process when you are thinking about seminaring at sea. The reason for this is that you are not choosing for yourself, alone. It is not just your own taste or budget that you are thinking about. You must think about your target audience first and foremost. If you are, in fact, going to get an audience either to offset your own expenses or to get hired as a guest presenter, you must match what you offer with what your customers want.

Choosing a destination becomes a very practical matter. If you are eager to cruise and speak, consider the most popular, shortest, and least expensive destinations for starters. Caribbean, Alaska's Inside Passage, and Mexico are three very popular cruise routes which make excellent seminar routes. It is very important for you to think about the whole package that your audience will be buying. If it is very expensive or exotic you automatically limit your audience. This is quite fine, if that is what you want to do. Just be aware in advance that if

---

Your Notes

you are anxious to conduct your seminar onboard a wonderful cruise ship tomorrow, choosing a $25,000 per person cruise to Antarctica probably isn't the place to start. In other words, think about your audience. Choose a destination, format, and price that will likely attract them. Then pack your bags and materials. Once you become experienced your destination and groups will grow to more luxurious ships and to more exotic destinations for longer periods of time.

Other Considerations When Choosing Your Destination

Once you have thought about who your audience is and narrowed the potential destinations, it is important to consider a few more issues, including:

1. How much actual seminar time do you want to have and really need? The problem is that if your seminar requires more time than you have, you may wind up losing your audience to various ports of call along the way. Start with the assumption that your program must fit into the trip's itinerary. Not the other way around.

Your Notes

2. Choose a cruise line capable of offering the best all-around support to you and your group participants. Remember, you will be judged not only the program you give but the entire system surrounding you. You will enjoy "virtue by association." But you can also suffer from the reverse.

3. Plan for the unplanned. We've all heard the expression, "life happens!" Plan the day and you can be sure life will plan it another way than you did. If this ever happens to you on land, you may be certain it will happen on the high seas. What this means is that you must always have a contingency plan ready to implement. Sometimes even the best plans go awry.

For example, on one of my own seminar at sea experiences aboard a five-star ship in the Caribbean, we were forced to change course in the middle of our trip due to threatening weather conditions. The ship diverted from our scheduled stop, Virgin Gorda, causing my precious seminar time to conflict with the snorkel and sting ray's shore excursion time in Aruba. Since I felt

---

Your Notes

compelled to stay with my original seminar schedule, I missed seeing both islands. Not surprisingly, half my class skipped out of class to visit Aruba!

4. Preview your potential ship. Unlike just a few years ago, it is very easy to learn about every corner of the cruise ship you are considering using. Most cruise lines have excellent websites and many provide you with a virtual tour of everything from stateroom to dining room, and more.

The following tips will help you gain insight and details about your prospective cruise ship:

A. Get on the internet, browsing the cruise line's web site.
B. Carefully read all the cruise line's promotional and group sales kits. These are very important because in many cases, your own participants will be seeing the same information you do. Be sure the pieces are up-to-date, persuasive, and accurate.

Your Notes

C. Ask your travel agent to order quantities of the cruise line's sleek color brochures, each filled with photos of the ships' public rooms, lounges, staterooms, and activity areas. The brochures will also contain pricing and other relevant information.

D. When possible, consider an actual site-visit onboard your prospective ship. Speak to as many of the hotel staff as possible. Listen carefully to what is said and even more importantly, feel the atmosphere. You want your own audience to be comfortable and sense they are welcome guests. Not just meal tickets. Remember, "virtue by association." To arrange your "scratch and sniff" test, talk with your travel agent to set up appointments with the staff before you go onboard.

E. Booking your cruise should take place as far out as possible. Very special events such as the Millennium cruises are booked out as much as five and even ten years! Begin planning now if you are interested in the summer of 2004 Olympics in Greece. Plan on booking

---

Your Notes

and making your deposit at least one year ahead to ensure getting the best stateroom locations and cabin selections along with your choice of sailing dates, early booking discounts, and even dining tables and times!

Last Minute Details:
Attention to a few last-minute details will help ensure your trip (and that of your group) is as successful and enjoyable as possible. Those details include:

1. Always take a copy of the written agreement between you and the cruise line along with you on the trip. Once your trip begins, you can't reach into your file-drawer and retrieve the document if there is ever a disagreement about any aspect of your role and/or what your group expects to receive. In some instances, once you set sail, your only means of communication with the outside "landed" world will be by over seas radio or via satellite phone service. Increasingly, however, many of the major cruise lines have

---

Your Notes

internet service available. If this is important to you, be sure to check it's availability out with hotel staff.

2. Always take proof of citizenship with you. If you don't have a current passport, then you must provide proof-of-citizenship documentation. In some cases, an original copy of your birth certificate will suffice. Check with your travel agent to confirm you are in possession of the right documents. There is no margin for error on this subject. I urge all my clients and seminar attendees to make photocopies of critical papers before sailing. Put the copies in a safe, yet easily accessible, place in case the originals are lost.

Some foreign nationals are required to provide "green-card" identification or special written authorization for passage into or through particular parts of the world. In some cases, these foreign nationals may board the ship but may not be able to disembark at certain ports if they don't have the right paper work. Don't assume all your participants are eligible for or are carrying U.S. Passports.

Your Notes

Your travel agent will provide a check list of necessary documentation, whether its passport, visa, or both.

Following is a sample listing of resources to telescope your process. Because each situation is different, the same information is not available for each cruise line. I am providing information that was made available to me at time of publication. For the complete Directory To Cruise Line's International contact Athina Press Publishing at the Travel Resource Center, Inc.

Address and telephone access:
Travel Resource Center, Inc.   PH: 503 232-5362
1630 S.E. Rex St.   Fax: 503 232-1952
Portland, OR 97202-6061
Website: http://www.seminaratsea.com

Your Notes

Cruise Line Contacts

AMERICAN CANADIAN CARIBBEAN CRUISE LINE

461 Water St. PH: (800)556-7450
Warren, RI 02885 FAX: (401)247-2350
Website: http://www.Accl-smallships.com
Guest Speaker Program: Yes
Program title: None
Requirements: Resume, video of speaking or performing your subject matter
Topics and speaker types: Educators, historians, destination experts of the area visited and light humor topics
Theme cruise program: None
Booking agents: Yes
Internet access: Yes
Ships: 3
Contact: Tricia Samson, Title: Assistant to the President, Marketing and Public Relations Department

Your Notes

CRYSTAL CRUISES

2049 Century Park East,   PH: (310)785-9300
Suite 1400   FAX: (310)286-9231
Los Angeles, CA 90067
Website: http://www.crystalcruises.com
Guest Speaker program: Yes
Program title: Crystal Vision Lecture Series
Topics and speaker types: Retired college professors emeritus, famous journalists, charismatic celebrities, best-selling authors, and well-known intellectuals and featured notables such as: Walter Cronkite, Caspar Weinberger, Edwin Newman, Arte Johnson, Bill Harris, Mary Rodgers, Judith Krantz, Michael & Pat York
Theme cruises: Yes
Annual Crystal Wine & Food Festival with gourmet events with Wolfgang Puck & Jacques Pepin.
Wine guests: Anthony Dias Blue & Bartholomew Broadbent
Booking agents: Yes
Internet access: Yes
Ships: 2
Contact: Mr. Kirk Frederick, Entertainment Director
Screens at least 100 applications per week. He is very happy to announce two exciting programs The *Crystal*

Your Notes

Enrichment Series and the *Crystal Computer University At Sea* being made available on every sailing year round with 22 personal computers aboard each of their two ships.

Crystal Enrichment Series: offers lectures on the destination, culture and maritime world capitals experts of the areas the ships visit, photography, computer programs, memoir writing tips, painting, art history.

Note: At time of printing nearly every one of this Line's sailings offers a wine and food event, e.g. *Crystal Wine & Food Festival/Great Chefs"*. Sign me up-Scotty!

CUNARD CRUISE LINES
6100 Blue Lagoon Dr.   PH: (305)463-3426
Suite 400   FAX: (305)463-3019
Miami, FL 33126
Website: http://www.cunardline.com
Guest Speaker program: Yes
Program title: None
Topics and speaker types: Human & public interest
Theme cruises: Yes
Booking agents: Yes
On board internet access: Yes
Ships: 5

Your Notes

Contact: Mr. David Stewartson, Title: Entertainment Director

Contact's comments: Fills over 750 lecture spots per year on five ships. The line works with ten plus various booking agents or suppliers. The booking agent gets paid a fee; the speaker does not. The speaker receives a gratis cruise or may even be required to pay a nominal daily fee of $50. The fee also depends on the caliber of speaker and/or the subject. If interested, send the relevant information directly to David Stewartson who will forward to booking agencies. This process is for all submissions.

HOLLAND AMERICA CRUISE LINE

300 Elliott Ave. West   PH: (206)281-3535
Seattle, WA 98119   FAX: (206)281-0351
Website: http://www.hollandamerica.com
Guest Speaker program: Yes
Program title: None
Topics and speaker types: Lecturers of celebrity status, famous people and novelists
Theme cruises: None
Booking agents: None
Internet access: None

Your Notes

Ships: 9
Contact: Cheryl Fluehr, Title: Entertainment Manager
Contacts comments: As of this printing the contact was not interested in offering much information about guest speaker requirements. Suggested whatever opportunities they have for speakers is very limited. Speakers only needed on Panama Canal and world voyage cruises. Targeting the senior market. For the 10+ day Panama cruise, they typically recruit Panama Canal or Mayan civilization experts.

RADISSON SEVEN SEAS
600 Corporate Dr.,   PH: (954)772-2283
Suite 410   FAX: (954)776-6123
Ft. Lauderdale, FL 33334
Website: http://www.rssc.com
Guest Speaker program: Yes
Program title: None
Topics and speaker types: Financial advisors, handwriting analysts, ports of call 'cruising the area' seminars
Theme cruises: None
Contact: Mr. Paul McEvoy, Title: Director of Entertainment
Booking agents: None

Your Notes

Internet access: None
Ships: 4
Contact's comments: Suggests the existing lecture programs are currently not too creative. They will be adding more innovative subjects and speakers soon.

Marketing Strategies That Produce Sell-Out Crowds

We know you've got a great speech or seminar. That's a given. Once you are in front of people, they love you. The trick, of course, is getting in front of them. Or in the case of getting your seminar on a great cruise, the issue most often is getting enough people so that all your expenses are paid with sufficient profit to make the experience a truly successful business venture. This section outlines strategies I have personally used for generating sell-out crowds. I know they work. While you will want to massage each of these to meet your own particular needs, the basic principles should be as powerful and effective for you as they have been for me.

Element One: Getting Group Leads

Filling your seminar slots is not something you want to do alone. You must build your team. I don't mean that

---

Your Notes

you have to go out and hire legions of sales' people. But you do need to get everyone who can support your effort involved – and rewarded. First on that team list are people I call "Group Leads." GL's are people who connect you to other key people within important organizations or networks.

Another category of support for you to think about are the people I call "Pied Pipers." The Pied Piper is someone who is directly connected to an organization and who will actively sign people up. The Pied Piper is your sales organization!

In addition to your own network and personal contacts, familiarize yourself with local chapters of national organizations. Your library will have a complete listing of major trade and professional associations. Each of these groups is a potential landing spot for your seminar at sea. The following short exercise will help you identify your most important basic resources for getting your seminar "off the ground," as it were:

Your Notes

Element Two: Gather Your Own Flock

Make a list here of your business associates, contacts and friends who are active members of a trade or professional organization or special-interest club. All are potential participants in your seminar at sea. Making this list will also quickly reveal potential sponsors, pied pipers and group leads.

Your list:
1
2
3
4

Define Your Target Market

If you aren't clear about who your market is, you'll never get to it. Ensure your success by listing key groups you would like to get to. Be specific.
(Example: members of Rotary, Chambers of Commerce, Optimist, attorneys, accountants, chefs)

Your Notes

> Your list:
> 1
> 2
> 3
> 4

My Customer Profile

Dr. Lynda Falkenstein[1] tells us that if we are really serious about getting business, we must do nothing less than "move in with our customers." I agree, figuratively of course. What this means is that you need to develop a detailed customer profile. In the space below list the key characteristics associated with your customer, e.g. age, income, life-style.

> Your list:
> 1
> 2
> 3
> 4

Your Notes

---

[1] Falkenstein, Dr. Lynda. *NICHECRAFT: Using Your Specialness to Focus Your Business, Corner Your Market, and Make Customers Seek You Out.* HarperBusiness, 1996.

Element Three: Hook-Up with a Sensational Travel Agent EXPERIENCED in Group and Cruise Travel

A significant factor in your overall success may well be your skill in connecting with an experienced travel agent. Experienced, that is, in group travel marketing, and negotiating with the cruise line reps. It is one thing to send one business person to a meeting. It is a whole other story to collect a group to go to that same event. Because of the TA's importance in your life at this point, I strongly suggest that you interview potential candidates. Make your list of criteria that you think your cooperating travel agent should bring to the party. Remember, that person will benefit substantially from working with you. Don't plan to settle. Following is my own basic criteria list.

Travel Agent Criteria List

- Experienced with group travel, especially seminaring, meeting planning, and the cruise industry
- Proven track record of success
- Bonded and registered with the state in which you are doing business

---

Your Notes

- Access to marketing materials important to your success
- Understands and connects to your seminar purpose and potential audience
- Pays due attention to your business by offering access to sales support, marketing, and materials critical to your success

⚓ *Special Note:*

Be sure to ask your travel agent about arranging co-op dollars to help pay advertising and other expenses.

Element Four: Get Sponsored!
The Best of All Worlds

Being sponsored by an organization can be the best of all worlds. In order to make this happen, you have to put your ultimate "win-win" hat on. Identify organizations that have a vested interest in the same target audience you have. Then you are going to approach key people in the organization, helping them understand how you can benefit their members AND the organization. The benefit may be exclusively educational, it may be financial, or it may be a combination of both.

Your Notes

The following tips will help you get your own sponsorships underway:

- Identify local affiliates of national organizations that conduct out-of-town meetings and conferences. Get involved with those key organizations. Your T.A. can help you here too! Once you are active, offer your speaking and seminar services to them on board ship as an alternative to a land-based program.
- Identify names of program and meeting planners associated with organizations on your "wish list" of potential sponsors. Since people move from job to job very frequently, you should call ahead to ensure that any promotional material you send will go to the right person. No one likes to get mail addressed to the last person who worked in the place.
- Once you have identified your key contact at the association, be sure you are very clear on the organization's target audience. You must know what the organization wants to accomplish from its meetings. Don't forget that the meeting planner's interest will be in satisfying his/her

---

Your Notes

audience. The meeting planner wants to look good. Get into that person's shoes and figure out what his/her world looks like. To help you get a jump-start on this, use the space below to list your client's "hot buttons." That is, what are the main concerns and interests of the person and/or organization you will be targeting. Remember, you have multiple levels of clients. The person who is hiring you is a client. The organization is a client. Their clients are their members and boards of directors.

Client   Hot Buttons
_____   _____
_____   _____
_____   _____
_____   _____
_____   _____
_____   _____
_____   _____

Your Notes

The following form will help you organize information about various groups' characteristics and needs.

Fact Finding:
An Organization Questionnaire

Organization Name_____
Today's date: ____/____/____
Type (Business, clergy, charitable)_____
Address: _____
City: _____
State: _____ Zip: _____
Phone: (___)_____-_____
Contact Person: _____
Title: _____
Size of membership: _____
Speaker program   Yes   No
Activities director   Yes   No
Newsletter: Yes   No
    If Yes, printed how often_____
Paid advertising: Yes   No
    If yes, where? _____
Volunteers: Yes   No
Past trips: Yes   No
Past cruises: Yes   No
Guest Speakers: Yes   No

===

Your Notes

Element Five: The Proposal and Sales Kit

Now that you have your contacts lined up and the qualifying information, you are ready to make your formal proposal. To telescope your success, I am including several examples of successful proposals right out of my own files. Again, you will want to massage these for your own situation, but keep in mind, the principles work, so don't alter the bones of the outline.

- *Who You Are* - your goal and what you are proposing
- *The Offer* – what benefits are in it for your sponsor
- *Responsibility Statement* - what you will do AND what you want your sponsor to do. CLARIFY!
- *Financial Projections & Budget* - how much you want to be paid, how that will happen, etc.
- *Complete Press Kit* – include samples of past seminars

Back up your proposal with a complete cruise sales kit including the free cruise brochures, sample promotional material and your press kit telling how wonderful you

---

Your Notes

are. These sales kits are provided by the cruise lines or your travel agent and can be enormously helpful in selling your seminar or speech to the potential group or contact. Of course, don't forget to have a formal written agreement ready when the cruise line extends it's invitation to you. I prefer simple, straightforward letters of confirmation and agreement instead of lengthy documents filled with technical language.

YOU'RE IT!

Of all the things to remember when you are marketing and selling your seminars at sea, none is more important than the "You're It" feature. If you are serious about getting sponsored by an outside organization and/or getting invited by a cruise line, whether for pay or trade or basic maintenance, you must remember that you are the product. People buy people. They are buying YOU. This means that all you can do to make yourself perceived as a celebrity will be critical to your seminar at sea success. What this means is that you must have a strong professional marketing plan in place well before you seek any kind of sponsorship.

Your Notes

While each of us must develop a marketing system appropriate for our own businesses, Dr. Lynda Falkenstein has outlined several strategies which I believe can be helpful for literally all professionals who ultimately want cruise lines to greet them with open arms. Following are just a few things she suggests to make yourself a household word and perceived as an even more valued commodity by your favorite cruise lines:

- Write a book
- Get on the speaking circuit
- Create a media plan which gets you on TV and radio talk shows
- Develop a column which appears in daily and specialized papers
- Contribute to newsletters published by key trade and professional publications
- Build a website that reflects who you are, what you stand for, and the value others see in what you do, e.g. testimonials!
- Get regular editorial coverage about what you are up to
- Get on every radio talk show imaginable

Your Notes

The bottom line is you must be a household word. The more visible you are, the more valuable you will be and the easier it will be for you to get your programs accepted by the cruise lines of your choice. Moreover, you will up your chances of getting them to call you instead of the other way around. And as we know all too well, when clients call you, the rules are entirely different.

A TRUE STORY ABOUT A SUCCESSFUL SELF-SPONSORED PROGRAM

You can always do it yourself. . . . .

Joe Lowe wanted to be a paid professional speaker and a world class business consultant based in the San Francisco area where he lives today. As a professional speaker, his desire was to hit the big time with fame and fortune. He wanted to be as big as the Tom Peters of the world. Unfortunately, he did not have a seminar topic or a focused business to offer any type of paid speaking or consulting services. He was passionate about his desire to be on the same speaker circuit as his role models.

Your Notes

Mary Long Harvey

Dec. 30, 1951 - April 11, 2010

Mary Long Harvey, 58, world traveler, educator and dance instructor from ballet to belly dancing, entered into eternal rest from complications associated with leukemia.

Mary also known as "Tots" and "Athena Maria" began traveling at the age of 16, joining her sister and family on a trip through Europe and the Middle East. She would continue her passion for people and cultures around the world.

As owner of Travel Resource Center, she wrote two travel books, "Travel Wise Travel Safe" and "Seminars at Sea." She also taught travel courses at Mt. Hood Community College and still had time to enjoy cooking, teach belly dance, love her cats and play golf at Eastmoreland Golf Course. She had conducted her own seminars on more than 100 separate cruises aboard the finest luxury liners traveling to every corner of the globe.

She was an amazing partner, sister, aunt and friend. She is survived by her life partner, Ron Irwin; stepchildren, Jacob and Autumn Harvey; brothers, George and Craig Cathey; and many nieces and nephews. She was predeceased by her husband, Paul Harvey; and sister, Colleen Sabri.

Services will be held at 1 p.m. Wednesday, April 21, 2010, in St. Agatha Catholic Church, 1430 S.E. Nehalem St., Portland, followed by a celebration of life and wake from 2:30 to 5:30 p.m. at Eastmoreland Golf Course, 2425 S.E. Bybee Blvd., Portland.

In lieu of flowers, please make donations to the American Cancer Society Research at www.cancer.org or 800-ACS-2345.

Please sign the online guest book at www.oregonlive.com/obits

Ginny went home to be with the Lord April 14, 2010. Her family is rejoicing that she is in heaven working in the garden with Jesus, her Lord and Savior, and all of her other loved ones that have gone before her.

Ginny was born in Blountville, Tenn. She moved to Oregon in 1958. She touched everyone's lives she came in contact with. Ginny, "Grandma M," was a kindred spirit and had a big heart and a kind word for everyone she met.

She proudly worked at Meier & Frank for 33 years, retiring in 2001. Her passion was taking pictures of flowers and imprinting beautiful poems on them. She loved sharing her prints with all who knew her.

She loved her sisters, children and grandchildren with all her heart. Ginny is survived by her sisters, Margie Cable and Marie Hutchens of Blountville; brothers, Clyde and Arthur Price of Bristol, Tenn; daughter, Patti de Carteret; and sons, Mike and Jeff. She has six beloved grandchildren, Nicolas, Alexandra, Matthew, Lara, Chet and Ella.

A memorial service will be held at 1 p.m. Wednesday, April 21, 2010, in Canby Evangelical

Eva Verle (Adams) Brown

March 20, 1923 - April 15, 2010

Eva passed away peacefully April 15, 2010, at West Hills Health and Rehabilitation Center, with family at her side.

Born March 20, 1923, Eva grew up in the Portland area and graduated from Franklin High School in 1941. She married Bill F. Brown June 29, 1941. After raising three children, Eva and Bill retired and began what would be almost 20 years of traveling all over the United States. After her husband's death in 2000, Eva began volunteering at the Oregon Zoo and spent the remainder of her life as a dedicated zoo volunteer.

Eva was preceded in death by her husband, Bill F. Brown Sr.; son, Thomas K. Brown; and grandson, Michael A. Clites. She is survived by her son, Bill F. Brown Jr.; daughter, Barbara A. Morrill; five grandchildren; 10 great-grandchildren; and two great-great-grandchildren.

The memorial celebration will be held at 2 p.m. Wednesday, April 21, 2010, in the Cascade

He came to a realization that until he found his focus, niched his business, and produced something of value (a publication, book or a manual) he would never make it. In order to get aboard he would have to become someone or something in demand. He decided to create his own platform and include himself as a prime speaker.
He finally – GOT IT!
He gathered the money from seminar investors and designed and implemented his own program. He setup an event, positioning himself as a top name speaker right there with the other keynote speakers. The idea was brilliant and the event was a huge hit. Joe fulfilled his dream and desires. He has now become one of them, a top name, on the speaking circuit and on cruise ships worldwide!

Moral of the Story:
If you don't have a group - create your own!

Your Notes

The Ultimate Fund-Raising Experience

It is no secret that fund-raising is not for the faint at heart. In today's world it seems everyone is out after the same dollars from the same people. Regardless of size, organizations are becoming more and more sophisticated and aggressive raising dollars to support their operations and causes. The bottom line is that competition is fierce for people charged with getting those charitable coffers filled. The beauty of seminaring at sea is that it is one of the best ways for an organization to raise money and make their niche at the same time!

Getting Your Foot in the Door
If fund-raising and cruising sound like a great combination to you, the news is good. There are many ways to get your foot in the door (more accurately put, on board a cruise ship). One of my own earliest and most successful experiences with fund-raising was aboard a fabulous cruise ship. Here's how I did it.

Living in a city where several of the world-class cruise ships come for dry dock and refurbishing, I knew there had to be opportunities to utilize these magnificent

---
Your Notes

vessels for fund-raising. I had to get my foot in the door, however. I made several contacts with major non-profit organizations. I looked for associations that had big goals with big corporate donors and a professional staff. The American Cancer Society met my criteria. My proposal also met theirs.

American Cancer Society Monthly Newsletter

CANCER CHRONICLE
Fall, 1995

WELCOME NEW STAFFERS!

The Oregon Division welcomes the following new staff people: Rowanna Carpenter, part-time Medical Affairs Assistant • Linda Hill, Executive Director, Central Area • Cherie Kistner, Special Events Director, Mid West Area • Erica Maxwell, Public Education and Volunteer Development Assistant • Peter McLean, Metro Public Education Program Assistant • Becky Minshull, Cars for a Cure Coordinator • Dave Rogers, Executive Director, Northwest Area • Steve VanAtta, Warehouse Manager • Cindy Lewis, part-time Cancer Helpline Assistant, is moving to full-time Program Director in the Northwest Area office.

CANCER REGISTRY UP AND RUNNING

Oregon finally joined the majority of other states in establishing a system for tracking cancer patients. The Cancer Registry Act, passed in 1995 by the Oregon Legislature, authorizes a registry to collect statistics on tumor types, dates of diagnosis, presence of tumor markers and where cancer patients live. This data collection allows researchers to track incidence of cancer, and even specific types of cancer by region and community. For instance, the statistics may reveal a higher incidence of breast cancer in particular areas of the state, allowing state health officials and researchers to investigate environmental, social and economic causes. Dr. Don Austin, an ACS volunteer, is the chief architect of the cancer registry. Oregon now becomes part of the National Cancer Registry established by Congress in 1992. The Centers for Disease Control and Prevention, a federal agency, will fund most of the cost of Oregon's cancer registry for at least the next four years.

CRUISE FOR A CURE

Ahhh... imagine yourself on a cruise ship. Close your eyes and think of the beautiful scenery, the relaxation, and of course the non-stop eating! Now imagine going on a cruise for a 30% discount, and having part of your fare benefit the American Cancer Society! This can happen when you book a cruise through Travel Resource Center. They offer trips to the sunny Caribbean, the wilds of Alaska, and almost anywhere else you dream up. There's even a trip available on the Queen Elizabeth 2. Call Travel Resource Center at 503/292-0755 for more information.

ANOTHER ACS NOBELIST

A California biologist renowned for his work on the genetics of fruit flies has been awarded the 1995 Nobel Prize in Physiology or Medicine. Dr. Edward B. Lewis is the 28th Nobelist supported by the American Cancer Society. He will share the Nobel Prize with two other scientists for discovering how genes control the early structural development of the body. Dr. Lewis received a $150,000 grant from the American Cancer Society in 1986. He used the ACS grant to study genetic regulation and development in Drosophila fruit flies, a project he started in 1946. His work led to crucial understanding of human development and the mechanisms underlying some genetic disease, including cancer.

In essence, together we co-sponsored and hosted 1,200 participants at $25 a ticket for ACS's annual winetasting event aboard Holland America's *SS Rotterdam* while it anchored in the Port of Portland, Oregon. The first year we raised $30,000 the first three hours tickets went on sale. The next year's event hosted 1,600 participants aboard their new ship, raising even more money. By sending a press release to our local television "Today Show" we were able to get the celebrity host to appear on the scene.

I am proud to say that after this door opened, my event and seminar business mushroomed and is, to this day, a significant part of my entire company. Much to my pleasure (and profit), I've maintained a close relationship with all the charitable groups with which I've had any fund-raising activity. To this day, I am still being sought after to conduct charity fund-raiser programs on board cruise ships all over the world.

Section Two contains many examples of proposals which I and other professionals have successfully used as the basis for our own major programming and events. I invite you to adapt them to your own situation and jump-start your own fund-raising on the high-seas.

Your Notes

Counting the Money

Setting fees and carefully costing out your seminar at sea is a critical step in making the whole experience successful. Especially if you are anticipating earning income from this activity, thoughtful numbers crunching is not an option. Even before the numbers' crunching, you need to determine what your specific purpose is in conducting your seminar at sea. Is it exclusively to get a free trip or is it to conduct your business activities and get paid for those as you would were you executing them on land? How you answer each of those will determine your course in setting fees and costing out your cruise experience.

Fee Setting Guidelines:
Following are some guidelines to help you set fees that will work for you and all involved in your seminars-at-sea.

1. First, and foremost, identify and work closely with a travel agent experienced in group travel. Your travel agent who should also be licensed

---

Your Notes

and bonded will handle all monies paid by participants. This is essential because your agent should be covered by an errors and omission insurance policy, something that is increasingly important in today's litiganeous society. In other words, if a mistake is made or problem happens along the way, your agent is covered. You aren't in the business of travel. Your agent is. You just happen to be using it to advance your business. Don't get in over your head.

If you have questions concerning your own liability when coordinating or participating in a group travel program, contact an insurance company specializing in travel agent needs.

2. Costing out your cruise is a fairly straightforward process. It is important to remember that when you put a group together, the group rate can be as much as 20% lower than the standard rack or published rates. If you are the organizer of the group, this leaves you a significant profit margin to work with. You can offer your cruise at a discount or offer at the standard published rate, depending upon your financial goals for the program.

Your Notes

In addition to the group discount available, most cruise lines pay travel agents between 10 and 20% commission for group bookings. This means you have yet more negotiating room with your travel agent. If you bring the whole package with little or no work for the agent, you are in a good position to negotiate a significant part of their standard commission.

The following breakdown illustrates the most common group pricing formula:

Brochure price, single fare:	$1,600
Group discount @ 15%:	less $240
Group discounted rate per person:	$1,360

Two other figures are very important:

Commission to travel agent @ 10%	$136
Available discount per person	$240

Where the Profit Is

By now you are beginning to see where the money is in group travel. With a group of 40, the above ticket would produce $15,040 in potential profits for someone. That someone may be you!

Your Notes

But as the presenter there is additional opportunity to generate revenue from your cruise. You are entitled to build in a professional fee for your speech or seminar. I suggest to my clients that they use the same formula in establishing that fee as they would were they conducting their program on land. After all, work is work and your brains are your livelihood. Your value doesn't change depending upon venue. If your fee for an eight-hour program on land is $295 per person, you've answered the question. It's $295 at sea. You may build that cost directly into the price of the ticket. That way, when people sign up for the cruise, they automatically get the program without seeing the fee which goes back to you. Or, you can show it as a separate line-item, offering it as an option. Personally, I prefer to bundle my program, not showing it as a separate line-item. When people sign-up, I'm automatically part of the package.

A Great Bonus!

A long-standing practice in the industry provides each of us with a great bonus opportunity. For every 15 people recruited to a cruise, you receive one free ticket. You may use that ticket any way you want. Give it to a

Your Notes

friend, take along your spouse or significant other. you can even sell it and make that part of the revenue stream.

☸ *Special Note:*

As a hired entertainer such as a singer, performer, dancer, comedian, or artist expect to sign at least a 13 week contract to work aboard just about any cruise line. Your round-trip air transportation, room, and board will be at the cruise line's expense. I've found the entertainer pay range is anywhere from $1200 - 6000 per month depending on level of experience and celebrity status.

Additional Revenue and Profit Opportunities

Presenting your seminar or program is the tip of the iceberg (figuratively speaking, of course) when it comes to revenue potential for those who seminar at sea. Following are just a few additional ways you can add handsomely to your income while cruising on the high seas:

1. Network your way to additional revenue. Check out what other programs in addition to your own are being presented. The social host or hostess can work with you on this. By meeting other

groups, you may be able to secure additional seminar engagements and/or meet key contacts for other programming.

2. Commission rebates can be an extremely lucrative source of income beyond your simple seminar fee. Consider presenting your travel agent a proposal whereby you receive an agreed-upon percentage of the gross revenue. You may fall into the classification of "outside sales agent." Ask your travel agent for details. Many travel agencies hire outside sales' agents. This status affords you the benefits of many discounts and upgrade opportunities which regular travel agents receive all the time.

3. Selling the "TC's" (tour conductor certificates and tickets) can be a significant revenue generator. As mentioned earlier, for every 15 seats sold in group tour, the 16th typically is free. You can use or sell it as you wish. Once I earned four freebies, sold them and netted $6,000 additional income.

4. Back of the room sales are another common and potentially lucrative revenue generator. For many speakers, this is, in fact, the real profit center. If

---

Your Notes

you prefer not to lug all your tapes, books, and other products on board, then a generous supply of order forms can accomplish the same thing.

5. Consulting and sale of your professional services are among the most pleasant side-benefits growing out of your seminar at sea experiences. Based on my personal experience over the years, I always anticipate a minimum of 20 hours fee-based consulting arising from any seminar I present, regardless of the number of attendees. Much of this consulting can occur right on board the ship in between sessions and ports of call. Some of my most favorite and lucrative consulting sessions have occurred on deck in the hot tub with the stars and moon as backdrop.

6. Scheduling back to back seminars is another way to increase your revenue with no additional cost for marketing and promotion. This is an easy thing to plan for once you know the entire cruise itinerary. Many cruise lines grant more time at sea, allowing you to complete your seminar schedule well before the cruise ends. On many occasion, I have literally jumped from one cruise ship to another after only three days, taking my

---

Your Notes

seminar materials with me, of course. The analogy you may be more familiar with is if you are accustomed to traveling from city to city to present the same seminar. What I do regularly is jump from ship to ship. Where I know many people who complain bitterly about living in austere impersonal hotels and racing through airports, I have never heard anyone complain about going from one luxury liner to another. One of the best things about this type of scheduling is that often times you save a great deal of time and money by not flying back and forth, avoiding buying additional and costly air tickets.

Special Note:

Always bring along an extra amount of order forms. There is only one copy machine on-board, and it may be un available. When people want to buy your products, you want to make it as easy and efficient as possible for them to write their name and visa number down.

On-Board Gratuities

No discussion of financials would be complete without considering the subject of tipping. This is very important

Your Notes

not just for you but for your group participants. If you are putting a group together, it will be your responsibility to alert them to the environment's expectations and protocols. The fewer surprises the better for everyone.

In essence, you and your group will tip. That's the expectation. If you as the group leader decide to handle all the tipping, it is essential that everyone understands that will be the case. If individuals are expected to do this on their own, it is equally important that they know this in advance so they can appropriately do their budgeting.

In most cases, the tipping process will occur accordingly:

> Tips are always paid at the end of each voyage. The night before disembarkation, you will receive a tip "cheat sheet," complete with appropriate envelopes. The "cheat sheet" lists how much you are expected to tip your assigned service waiters. You can anticipate that your "cheat sheet" will include typical suggestions such as: dining room waiter $5-7, busperson $3-4, cabin or room

steward $5-7. Remember, these are on a **PER DAY** basis. If your cruise is 5 days, you tip each service person for each day.

In addition to the people receiving tips for each day of the cruise, you will want to tip for special services received. For example, the wine steward typically receives 10-15% of the group's bill. The restaurant manager or maitre d' are not to be forgotten. A 15% gratuity is automatically applied to all service in lounge areas, so your waiters and bartenders are covered for basic tips. If you have enjoyed particularly excellent or service beyond-the-call, I encourage you to remember those individuals who provided it with a little extra.

Especially if you ever intend to return to the same line, it is very important to leave a courteous and to the extent you believe the service deserves, a generous tip. I can personally attest to the fact that on repeat voyages (as well as totally new cruises) I've experienced the pleasure of having the same waiters. Trust me. They do remember who tips and who does not.

Your Notes

⚙ *Special Note:*

One of the special advantages of traveling on the more luxurious cruise ships is that the more expensive your trip, the less tipping you'll do. In fact, on five-star or more cruises there is no tipping at all. To ensure you don't miss a beat on this one, check out the guidelines with your cooperating travel agent.

Frequently Asked Questions
(with Answers)

Can I call home?

You can communicate from the ship-to-shore to virtually anywhere in the world via the ship's satellite system. You can't simply pick up the phone in your cabin and dial home without having made prior arrangements with the ship's radio room, which is usually located on the top deck near the bridge. Normally, I go directly to the radio room and make my calls from there.

Calls can't be made when the ship is sitting in port or docked. Due to international law, you must be a few

---

Your Notes

miles out to sea. When you are in port, you can call from a telephone booth or a phone station.

☼ *Special Note:*

Calling from the ship can be very expensive. Be sure to check the rates before making a call or sending a fax.

Can I get on the internet or check email?

The cruise lines are adding on-line access to their fleet of ships for passengers and crew with increasing frequency. It is wise to contact the line directly for their updated information. If your ship does not yet have this feature, you can get on-line access while the ship is at port by going to a local business that offers on-line services.

Am I able to stay current with the news?

Most of the newer ships have television in each of the staterooms. Some of them feature a central television viewing room where CNN and other top news stations run throughout the day. Each evening before retiring you receive the ship's daily agenda with updated world news and events in your stateroom.

Your Notes

What is the average length of a seminar-at-sea cruise?

Three, four, or seven day voyages to the Caribbean, Mexico, and Greek Islands are most typical and best for seminars or meetings at sea. Alaskan cruises are usually a minimum seven day voyage, while Mediterranean Voyages (to/from Spain, Italy, or Greece) are typically 10-12 days in duration.

Is there a typical seminar-at-sea group size?

Groups range from 20-200 participants depending on popularity or demand. Remember, you must have a minimum of 15 fully paid passengers to earn your freebie. When you get into 400+ attendee's, you enter into a partial charter situation with a totally different ball game.

Can I bring visitors aboard?

In order to have visitors aboard while in any port you must have visitor passes available. To do this, contact the cruise line's main office and request a visitor's pass well in advance of your trip. Be aware that in some ports, visitors are strictly prohibited.

Your Notes

What kind of arrangements can be made if someone in my group is celebrating a special occasion?

On nearly every cruise, someone will have a birthday, be celebrating a wedding anniversary, or some other special occasion. Cruise lines go beyond their call of duty by making the occasion very special. They will often provide "free" cakes, unusual pastries, party favors, and a festive atmosphere for you and your group---all free of charge!

How do I know a seminar-at-sea format will work for me and my audience?

The only way to really know if seminaring at sea fits your style and focus is to give it a shot. Invest in a 3-4 day mini-cruise sailing out of Miami to the Bahamas or sail round-trip from Los Angeles to Mexico. After just a few days, you'll know if more seminars at sea are in your future.

What should I pack?

Without a doubt, this is the most frequently asked question. Interestingly it is men who most often want to know what they should take along on the cruise. In nearly all cases, common sense will be your best guide in answering this questions. Consider the category of cruise, type of seminar you'll be conducting, and the destination. Obviously you'll pack differently for a trip to the Bahamas than you would for a trip to Alaska. Most importantly, during seminars expect to wear "business casual" attire as you would during your regular work week. Casual dress is fine while in port and after seminar hours.

Can I take along family members or companions?
Usually you can take whomever you want depending on your sponsor or role. You are allowed up to four passengers in a quad cabin.

What if I get sea sick?
Due to the size, design and the use of stabilizers, people rarely suffer from seasickness. If you are prone to motion sickness then consider the myriad of remedies in the market place. It is highly recommended you check with your physician prior to setting sail to get a few sample remedies to take along with you. The sundries shop may

---

Your Notes

be closed on board when you have urgent need for these remedies. Here are a few of the more common treatments:

- Transdern Scop – The travel patch. Peel off patch worn behind your ears stays absorbed for up to three days. By prescription only.
- Seabands – Two elastic wrist bands worn three inches from where your wrists and palms connect. Designed on the principle of accupressure and are drug free.
- Dramamine, Bonine – Similar over the counter products. Small pill taken prior to, and during travel.

Can I stay in port before or after the cruise?

Yes, it is advisable to be at port before your group and ship arrives. This is called a pre or post cruise overnight hotel stay. In fact, sometimes the overnight stays are mandatory before cruising.

Special Note:

When traveling from the west coast to the east coast, cruises leave Florida at 5:00pm to the Caribbean and Bermuda. This means that for a 7 day voyage, you will be away at least 8 days / 7 nights. If you are trying to

---

Your Notes

minimize your time away, take a red eye flight and arrive at least two hours prior to departure. Also, check out east and west coast repositioning cruises offering 2-3 days at sea from New York to the Bahamas, or Vancouver B.C. to Los Angeles every spring and fall.

What kind of tax deductions or travel benefits are available?

Always check with your CPA for business travel tax deductions and guidelines. When I became immersed in this business, my accountant was delighted to tell me that all my travel and related expenses are deductible. Keep detailed and accurate account of all your expenses. Most-often, your travel expenses will be deductible providing the are "directly related to" the trip before, during, and after. In the past, business travel expenses have been 100% deductible where meals and entertainment have been 80% deductible. The variables are many, and there are no printed foolproof guidelines for me to offer. I strongly recommend that you work with a knowledgeable accountant. Also you should order the FREE IRS guidelines that include information on "luxury travel."

Your Notes

⚓ Special Note:

For free IRS information call 1(800)829-3676 for Publication #463, *Travel, Entertainment, and Gift Expenses.* They will mail, fax, or email you the information.

⚓ Special Note:

Get the foreign currency exchange rates documented before leaving the USA. I always attach the rate to my income tax records before giving it to my accountant. This eliminates any confusion on the exchange rate at the time I was doing business in a foreign port.

Your Notes

Your Seminaring-at-Sea Vocabulary

By taking your seminars and programs to sea, you are literally entering another culture. Another world with a language all its own. Following is a listing of key terms to help you navigate within your new culture without a hitch.

AFFINITY GROUP: An association or group formed and brought together for the same interests

AFT: Back or rear of the ship

AIR ADD-ON: Air transportation to and from the ship

BERTH: A stateroom bed. Also a dock or slip where a boat or ship docks at a pier

BLOCKED SPACE: A reserved and confirmed number of seats or staterooms

BOOKING: A reservation process to confirm a seat, berth, or stateroom

---

Your Notes

BOW: Forward or the front of the ship

BRIDGE: Glass area in front where the ship is commanded, navigated and steered. The Captain's work area

CABIN STEWARD: A housekeeping person in charge of cleaning your stateroom

CATEGORY: A grading system for staterooms

COMMISSION: Money paid to the travel agents and others for selling travel services. Usually a percentage of the total cost

CROW'S NEST: Platform at the top of the mast. Used for lookout

DISEMBARKATION: Exiting the ship

EMBARKATION: Entering the ship

FIRST SEATING: The first of the two meals served on the ship

Your Notes

GANGWAY: Railed platform or ramp used for people to get on and off the ship

GATEWAY CITY: Hub cities from which most passengers travel to get to the cruise

GRATUITY: Tips given to shipboard personnel for services received by passengers

GUARANTEED SHARE PROGRAM: A set price paid by a single cruise passenger that may or may not be a shared cabin or stateroom with another person

HELM: Usually where the ship's wheel and steerage are located

HOST: Person in charge of the group at certain times

INDEPENDENT CONTRACTOR: Self employed person who is hired on a per-project basis or who has many clients. Not employed by anyone else. Check IRS definition to determine if you qualify for this status.

Your Notes

INSIDE CABIN: A stateroom on a ship without a porthole or outside view.

LOG: Official record of the days activities

LOWER BERTH: The lowest bed to the ground on a ship

MANIFEST: Passenger, crew and cargo lists

MUSTER STATION: Gathering point where life boat drill and supplies are held

OPTION: Paid passenger fare but the cruise line may upgrade to a higher option (category). Passenger decides which to take.

OUTSIDE CABIN: A stateroom with a porthole for a window. Allows you to have a view of the outside.

PORT CHARGES & TAXES: A charge or government port tax collected by the cruise ship from the passengers. Paid to travel agent at final payment.

Your Notes

PORTS OF CALL: Schedule of ports where a ship stops on a set itinerary

PORT SIDE: The left side of the ship as you face the bow

PROOF OF CITIZENSHIP: Birth certificate, passport or voter's registration documents

PURSER: Ship's employee in charge of passenger services

REGISTRY: The country to which the ship is registered. The ship is governed by the laws of the country to which is registered. It also must follow the laws of the countries it visits.

SECOND SEATING: The second of the two meal sittings

SHORE EXCURSION: Local sight-seeing tour on land offered in addition to the cruise

---

Your Notes

SINGLE OCCUPANCY: Single person in a stateroom or cabin even though it could be shared with someone else

STARBOARD: The right side of the ship as you face the bow (front)

STATE ROOM: A cabin on a cruise ship

STEWARD: A cruise ship's employee. Works for the ship's housekeeping or food & beverage departments

TENDER: A smaller boat (sometimes the ship's lifeboats) that transport passengers and supplies to and from the anchored ship in harbor to port.

TOUR DESK: An information desk on board the ship. The place where passengers buy shore excursions on board.

TOUR ESCORT: Designated person who goes with the group, assisting passengers needs

---

Your Notes

TOUR LEADER: Person in charge of the entire group and all its needs

TOUR ORGANIZER: Person who creates and secures the group, takes the money and works with the travel agency

TOURIST CARD: A temporary entrance card allowing travelers in and out of countries. Similar to a visa.

TRANSFERS: Transportation provided from point A to point B such as from the airport to the ship

UPGRADE: To move up to a better category of service.

UPPER BERTH: Like a bunk bed. The top bed in a stateroom

Your Notes

Part Two

Cruise Ship Profiles, Deck Plans, & Photo Gallery

This section contains photographs to show you bitesize glimpses of life on board the cruise ships with a particular focus on what is not shown or told in the cruise lines glossy brochures. These photos were also chosen to help you enjoy your armchair voyage from the conference room to the captains table. Bon voyage!

REGENCY CRUISES
Captains dinner table aboard the *Regent Sea*. Mary Long seated 1st on right hand side
Photo courtesy of TRC, Inc.

AMERICAN CANADIAN CARIBBEAN LINE, INC.
Trish Samson, Seminar speaker abord the *Nantucket Clipper*
Photo courtesy of American Canadian Caribbean Line, Inc.

COSTA CRUISE LINES
Conference room aboard the *Costa Romantica*
Photo courtesy of Costa Cruise Lines

RADISSON SEVEN SEAS CRUISES
Guest lecture aboard the m/s *Song of Flower*
Photo courtesy of Radisson Seven Seas Cruises

RADISSON SEVEN SEAS CRUISES
Ship tender of the *Paul Gauguin* taking the passengers from ship to shore in Tahiti
Photo courtesy of TRC, Inc.

RADISSON SEVEN SEAS CRUISES
The showroom used for seminars aboard the *Paul Gauguin*
Photo courtesy of TRC, Inc.

COSTA CRUISE LINES
Conference room aboard the *Costa Victoria*
Photo courtesy of Costa Cruise Lines

MEDITERRANEAN SHIPPING CRUISES
Large showplace room used for seminars aboard the *MV Rhapsody*
Photo courtesy of Mediterranean Shipping Cruises

CAPE CANAVERAL CRUISES
Café Miramar of *Cape Canaveral* used for seminars and large conferences
Photo courtesy of Cape Canaveral Cruises

RADISSON SEVEN SEAS CRUISES
Paul Gauguin ship anchored in Tahiti
Photo courtesy of TRC, Inc.

CONDUCTING SEMINARS AT SEA

RADISSON SEVEN SEAS CRUISES
Mary Long toasting the Hotel Manager, Mr. Oliver Hammerer at the Captain's Welcome Aboard Party aboard the *Paul Gauguin* in Tahiti

Photo courtesy of TRC, Inc.

HOLLAND AMERICA LINE Mary Long with the ships chief officer during the 1st in the nation American Cancer Society's fund-raiser aboard a cruise ship. Flagship of the line aboard the *Rotterdam* in Portland, Oregon   Photo courtesy of TRC, Inc.

RADISSON SEVEN SEAS CRUISES
Mary Long ready to board the unique 26' draft catamaran
Radisson Diamond in San Juan, Puerto Rico
Photo courtesy of TRC, Inc.

RADISSON DIAMOND

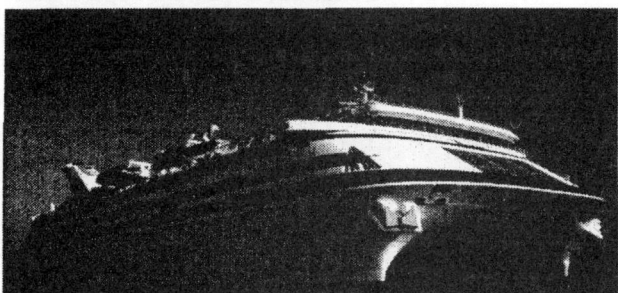

FACILITIES
Computer Rooms
Conference Center
Concierge
Duty Free shop
Golf Range
Health Spa/Salon
In-house Publishing Center
Jacuzzi
Jogging Track/Vita Course
Laundry/Dry Cleaning/Valet Service
Medical Center
Photo Shop
Retractable Floating Marina
Room Service (24-hour)
Safes in suites
Satellite Telephone Service
Skydeck Heliport
Swimming Pool
Underwater Viewing Room

PUBLIC ROOMS
The Grand Dining Room
The Grill (casual restaurant)
Splash Bar (pool bar)
The Club (quiet lounge)
Chips (casino)
Windows (lounge)
Constellation Center (conference area)
Boardrooms A, B, C
Rooms I, II, III, IV, V, VI
  (breakout rooms)

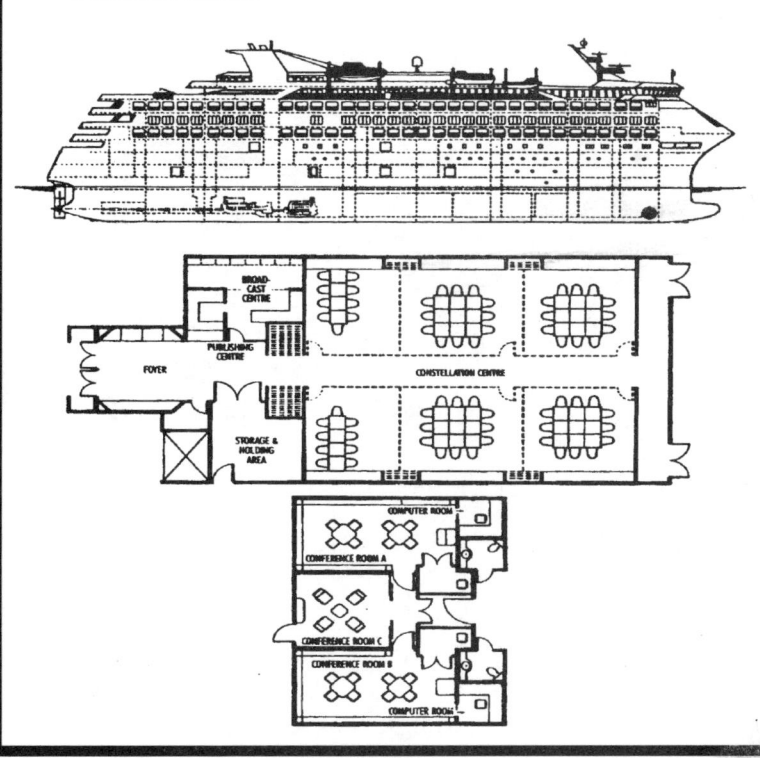

OCEANBREEZE

PUBLIC ROOM CAPACITIES

Pacific Card Room*/Library	31
Five Star Disco	
Seat capacity	90
Reception style	120
Mayfair Lounge	
Seat capacity	88
Reception style	100
Cafe Miramar*	
Seat capacity	160
Reception style	180
The Theatre*	120
Rendezvous Lounge*	
Seat capacity	400
Reception style	500
Caravelle Dining Room	440
Executive Board Room*	15

* Can be used as meeting facilities.

FACILITIES

- Beauty Salon & Massage Therapy
- Children's Room
- Fitness Center
- Full Casino
- Fully Air Conditioned
- Heated Swimming Pool
- Laundry Service
- Medical Facilities
- Movie Theater
- Postal Service
- Radio Room
- Safety Deposit Boxes
- Sauna
- Whirlpool

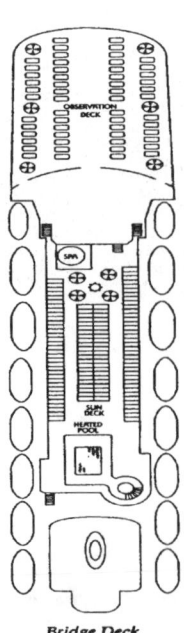

Bridge Deck

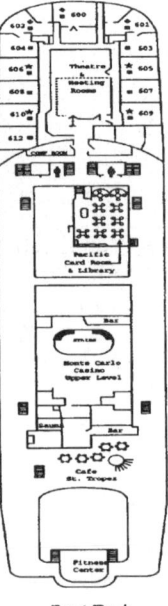

Boat Deck

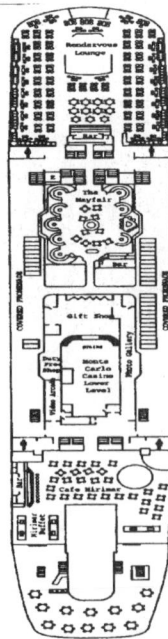

Promenade Deck

CLIPPER CRUISE LINE
Snorkel break near the *Nantucket Clipper* in the tropics
Photo courtesy of Clipper Cruise Line

CLIPPER CRUISE LINE
Whale watching (added attraction) during a seminar break from the *Nantucket Clipper*
Photo courtesy of Clipper Cruise Line

AMERICAN CANADIAN CARIBBEAN LINE, INC.
Disembarking aboard the *Niagara Prince* in the tropics
Photo courtesy of American Canadian Caribbean

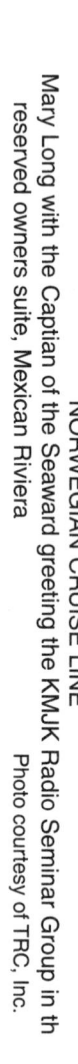

NORWEGIAN CRUISE LINE
Mary Long with the Captian of the Seaward greeting the KMJK Radio Seminar Group in th reserved owners suite, Mexican Riviera
Photo courtesy of TRC, Inc.

KMJK RADIO
Invites You To Join Our
'FUN IN THE SUN

CRUISE & CONFERENCE'

April 1 – 4, 1995
ABOARD NORWEGIAN CRUISE LINE'S
M/S SOUTHWARD

ITINERARY: Los Angeles, Catalina Island, San Diego, Ensenada/Mexico, Los Angeles

INCLUDES: Roundtrip airfare from your home city to Los Angeles, CA., Cruise berth, port tax, RT airport transfers to the port All meals, beverages and entertainment aboard ship
Not included: Shore excursions, shopping charges on board or in port and extended hotel stays before or after the cruise

REGISTRATION: Mail or fax the attached sign up form directly to KMJK Radio sales department.

All travel arrangements are provided by Travel Resource Center, Inc. Retail Travel Division.
Ph: 800 381–6000 or (503) 292-0755

Flyer for KMJK Radio 'Fun in the Sun' Cruise and Conference
Flyer courtesy of TRC, Inc.

CLIPPER CRUISE LINE
Seminar taking place in the lounge aboard the *Yorktown Clipper*
Photo courtesy of Clipper Cruise Line

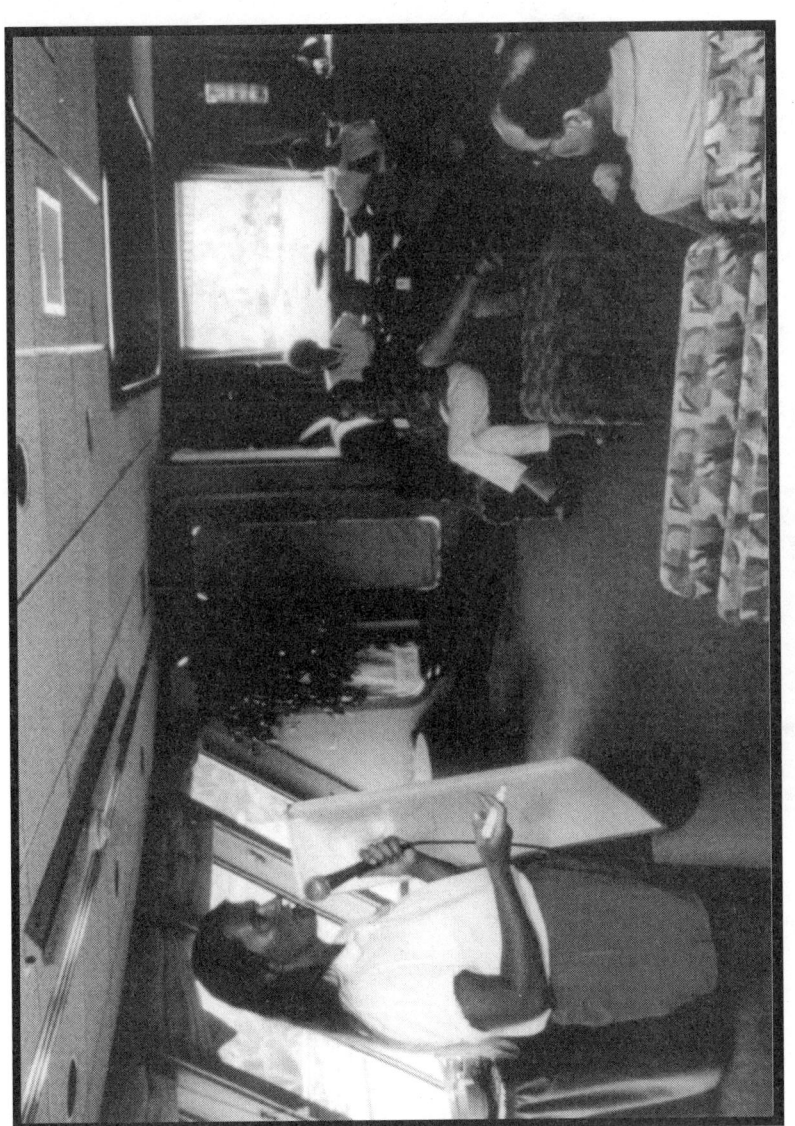

CLIPPER CRUISE LINE
Guest lecture presenting aboard the *Nantucket Clipper*
Photo courtesy of Clipper Cruise Line

REGENCY CRUISES
Seminar-at-sea group taking a stretch on deck in Alaska aboard the *Regent Sun*
Photo courtesy of TRC, Inc.

Queen Elizabeth 2

CRUISE TO HAWAII

Aboard the legendary *QUEEN ELIZABETH 2*
JANUARY 18 - 23, 1997
American Cancer Society Annual Fundraiser Cruise Benefit

ITINERARY

January 18, Thurs	Fly Portland-Los Angeles or San Diego, Motorcoach transfer to Ensenada, board the QE2 to sail at 5:00pm
January 19, Fri	Day at Sea - Rest and Relaxation
January 20, Sat	Day at Sea - Dance til' dawn
January 21, Sun	Day at Sea - QE 2 famous SPA AT SEA
January 22, Mon	Arr 8:00am Lahaina, Maui - full day in Maui, depart 11 PM
January 23, Tue	Arr Honolulu 8:00am to disembark the ship, transfer to the airport for return flight home or stay to enjoy Hawaii

	Price	Cabin category	
Prices from:	$1267	M5	Outside upper/lower
	$1337	M4	Inside
	$1407	M3	Inside
	$1540	MM	Outside
Port tax add'l: $212.50	$1806	C4	Outside
Includes RT airport transfers	$1946	C3	Outside

A portion of your cruise ticket cost will benefit the American Cancer Society.
For reservations call: 503 292-0755

AMERICAN CANCER SOCIETY
Promotional Flyer for Annual Fundraiser Cruise Benefit aboard the
Queen Elizabeth 2   Flyer courtesy of TRC, Inc.

CUNARD CRUISE LINE Captain's Welcome Aboard Party 'Cure For Cancer' sailing to Hawaii aboard the QE2. Sponsored by TRC, Inc. and American Cancer Society (ACS). Mary Long on right with Mr. David Gilley, President ACS and wife Roberta Gilley. Photo courtesy of TRC, Inc.

TRAVEL RESOURCE CENTER, INC.

6443 S.W. Beaverton-Hillsdale Hwy., Ste. 390• Portland, OR 97221
Phone 503-292-0755• Fax 503 292-2294

February 4, 1995

David Gilley, Director
American Cancer Society
0330 S.W. Curry St.
Portland, OR 97201

RE: EXECUTIVE COMMITTEE SEMINAR AT SEA VOYAGE

Travel Resource Center, Inc. (TRC) proposes to arrange the ACS Oregon Chapter along with the national committee offer their annual conference with a seminar at sea venue aboard Cunard Lines *'Sagafjord'*. This five star cruise ship will arrive in Port of Portland as part of her repositioning voyage enroute to Alaska for the summer season. The ship departs Portland, Oregon May 13th to arrive in Vancouver, B.C. Canada on May 15, 1996. As the executive committee member headlining the seminar I propose my keynote topic be *How To Conduct Profitable Fund-raisers Aboard Cruise Ships*. This event held aboard Cunard Line will be a perfect stage setting for the meeting.

BENEFITS
- ACS will receive a portion of the profit as a gift donation from the sale of each air/sea ticket following the cruise in the form a check from TRC.
- ACS will have an opportunity to enjoy the benefits of a cruise conference
- Seminars and meetings are held on a world class luxury liner
- ACS will receive one free air/sea ticket for each 16 full paid passengers

TRC WILL PROVIDE
- Assistance with promotional and advertising assistance
- Secure co-op funding arrangements with their travel agency affiliation
- I am pleased to offer my seminar, services and efforts once again as part of the ACS Executive Committee benefit package

ACS WILL PROVIDE
- Direct mailings to the Oregon committee members
- Direct mailings to the national board members
- Secure underwriter to pay keynote speakers fee and expenses

We look forward to confirming this proposal and getting under way soon for this exciting opportunity and event.

Regards,

Mary Long
President

Letter to David Gilley of the American Cancer Society
Letter courtesy of TRC, Inc.

PETE'S BREWING COMPANY
Group photo on deck of Carnival Cruise Lines Jubilee. Founder, Pete Slosberg back row standing 6th from the left.
Photo courtesy of Pete's Brewing Company

NORWEGIAN CRUISE LINES
Seminar-at-sea group photo on deck in the Caribbean aboard the *m/s Seaward*
Mary Long 6th from left lower deck.
Photo courtesy of OSSN

About the Author

Mary Long is founder and president of Travel Resource Center, Inc., a company specializing in travel education, training and consulting. Since 1987, her seminar business and workshops have taken her on hundreds of cruises to 38 countries. Mary is the world authority consulting over 7000 participants from Fortune 500 companies to individuals how-to take advantage of working vacations on the high seas to exotic destinations.

Mary hosts television, radio and tele-class seminars on behalf of the travel industry in the U.S.A. and abroad. Today, Mary's passion is sharing her level of expertise and enthusiasm for the enjoyment of others so they, too, can experience the endless rewards from their own exciting seminaring-at-sea venue.

Note From the Author

As I work on the revised edition of this book I invite you to send me your seminar at sea experiences either as a participant or a speaker. Your story will be included (permission granted) in the next edition along with your sample sales, promotional materials and seminar agendas. By sharing your experiences, the readers will gain insightful and timely information to help them attain successful seminars at sea. In addition, my company Travel Resource Center, Inc. is developing a 'Seminar at Sea' speaker organization that will be directly linked with my website. The organization will be a great resource for associations, organizations and cruise lines interested in hiring qualified speakers. If you are interested, please send your information to:

Athina Press Publishing
1630 S.E. Rex St.
Portland, OR 97202-6061
or via Email to: marylong@travelresourcecenter.com

Order Form

Directory to Cruise Lines International

This is your resource and contact guide to the cruise lines worldwide. This complete directory is updated annually. Listings include all of the following information:

Cruise Line name	Addresses	Phone/Fax
Booking Agent Information	Fleet Information	Key Contact
Entertainment Director	Sample Deck Plans	Website
Conference Room Profile	Destinations/Itineraries	Equipment Data
Guest Speaker Program	Guest Lecture Program	Theme Cruises

Detach and return this order form with your payment today!

Directory to Cruise Lines International - $22.95 + $3 shipping per book

Select method of payment: ☐ Check enclosed   Check # _____
                          ☐ MasterCard   ☐ Visa

Credit Card #:_____   Expires:___/___

Signature:_____

Name:_____

Address:_____

City:_____ State:_____ Zip:_____

Mail or fax your order form to: Athina Press Publishing
Fax: (503)232-1952 Ph: (503)232-5362 1630 SE Rex St.
Website: http://www.seminaratsea.com Portland, OR 97202-6061

Your Notes

Your Notes

Your Notes

Your Notes

Your Notes

Your Notes

Your Notes

Your Notes

Your Notes

Your Notes

Your Notes

Your Notes

Your Notes